OUTCOMES OF A
FORTUNE
COOKIE

OUTCOMES OF A FORTUNE COOKIE

Here's to "Cracking Open" Good fortune in 2020!

Love,
Jill Gandy
2019

JILL GANDY

Copyright © 2019 by Jill Gandy.

Library of Congress Control Number:	2019915988
ISBN: Hardcover	978-1-7960-6496-4
Softcover	978-1-7960-6495-7
eBook	978-1-7960-6494-0

All rights reserved. No part of this book may be reproduced or transmitted in any form or by any means, electronic or mechanical, including photocopying, recording, or by any information storage and retrieval system, without permission in writing from the copyright owner.

The views expressed in this work are solely those of the author and do not necessarily reflect the views of the publisher, and the publisher hereby disclaims any responsibility for them.

Any people depicted in stock imagery provided by Getty Images are models, and such images are being used for illustrative purposes only.
Certain stock imagery © Getty Images.

Print information available on the last page.

Rev. date: 10/10/2019

To order additional copies of this book, contact:
Xlibris
1-888-795-4274
www.Xlibris.com
Orders@Xlibris.com
804131

CONTENTS

Introduction vii

#1: If you want the rainbow, you must first tolerate the rain 1
#2: When in doubt, Be yourself 5
#3: A distant relationship is beginning to look more promising 8
#4: Success is a journey, not a destination 12
#5: Be willing to assert yourself in situations of great importance 16
#6: Your warmth radiates upon those around you 19
#7: · Travel with an open heart and positive expectations 24
#8: Work on improving your exercise routine 28
#9: The best angle from which to approach any problem is the 'TRY'-angle 31
#10: You will be changing your present line of work 34
#11: Investigate the new opportunity that will soon become an option 39
#12: You will discover something fun from your investments this month 42
#13: Truth? You CAN handle the Truth! 45

Peace of Poetry: The Fortune Cookie 48

#14: The Self-Proclaimed Fortune: The ability to talk to yourself is a well needed dialogue to put truth into perspective..50
#15: Your respect for others will be your ticket to success 53
#16: Past Inspirations and Experience will be Helpful in Your Job 56
#17: You should enhance your feminine side at this time 59
#18: Someone is speaking well of you..62
#19: Be willing to take advice as to give it. 65
#20: Your Love Life will be Happy and Harmonious 68
#21: Something on four wheels will soon be a fun investment for you..71
#22: A pet will grace your presence 75
#23: Give small gifts of yourself as if to never receive anything in return..78
#24: Good health will be yours for a long time..............................81
#25: You will lead a comfortable life..85
#26: Follow your heart for success in the coming week..................89

INTRODUCTION

On special occasions such as birthdays and award achievements, my family and I love to celebrate by going out to eat at our local Hibachi restaurant.

As we are invited in and seated around the over-sized rectangular grill, we contemplate the deliciousness of the up and coming meal along with the entertainment of the 'Happy Cook' of the day. Will it be the steak, the chicken, or the shrimp hibachi that will be enticing our taste buds? How about white or fried rice to begin filling our bellies as the veggies take a little longer to sauté? Hummm, such appetizing questions. So, are you hungry?

All is fine and good as the conversation around the table is underway about why we are here in the first place. But the adventure hasn't even begun yet.

It is at the end of the meal, and the server is on their way with the check and a hand full of the ever-mysterious fortune cookies that are ready to reveal their hidden secrets.

We pay for the meal and reach out our hand to take the cookie that is closest to us. Crack!

"Many seek you out for insightful advice."

Oh, will they now, Mr., Mrs, and/or Ms. Fortune Cookie! Your wisdom can be so cryptic.

This book is dedicated to
Emma and Joshua Gandy

In hopes that when I am gone,
They will have something to look back and remember…
My humor, My happiness, and My love.
I love you both so much, Mom.

#1

If you want the rainbow, you must first tolerate the rain

Let us sit down together and not talk about the rainbow but talk about the rain. The rainbow is a given. Scientists explain it as being light that is separated into its colors by the water in the atmosphere. Believers explain it as a sign from God to never destroy life on earth again. However, the rain can come in many forms such as a slow and steady downpour that saturates the ground like a monsoon, a whirlwind like a hurricane causing havoc and devastation, a brilliant darkening of the sky with flashes of light like a thunderstorm, and the life changing convergence of all three in a perfect storm. For a beloved family member (BFM), I was ever present to witness a hurricane-like rain while keeping an eye on the rainbow.

My immediate family does a lot of camping, but we also like to cruise. My husband and I took our first cruise in early 2002. We were accompanied by my mom, dad, sister, and a close aunt and uncle. Six wonderful days of no cleaning, cooking, or driving long distances was the selling point. I, also, loved coming back to our small room after dinner to find little chocolates laying on our pillows and the towel-folded animals on our bed. Since then, my immediate and extended family have continued this style of vacationing because it has been the best bang for our buck.

We normally gather a consensus among those who have cruised with us before; to check schedules and available dates and start planning the next adventure at least a year in advance. While planning our latest cruise, my Beloved Family Member called me to tell me that she was receiving some extra cash from her tax return, so I mentioned that she and my niece should come on the cruise. She was all for it, and we booked them a room on the same deck.

During the booking process, she gave me her passport information and said that she would use my niece's birth certificate as proof of US citizenship. After all that was said and done, they had their room, boarding passes, and luggage tags ready for an epic adventure.

When there are so many of us traveling together, we like to leave out of a nearby port because it lowers our vacation costs since we can simply drive instead of fly. We plan to head toward the port on a Saturday, so we don't have to rush Sunday morning to check in for boarding.

While going through our paperwork and documentation together Friday night, my BFM had her passport but was unable to find my niece's birth certificate. After the realization of not having it, a look of shear panic shot through her eyes like a bolt of lightning knowing that my niece could not get on the boat without it. I stood there helpless and watched as the dark clouds gathered around her and ripped the joy from her grasp.

For the past 23 years that I have known her, her pendulum of luck can swing from amazing to tragic in mere seconds. Her resilience to tragedy is a miracle in itself. Throughout the next fourteen hours, she frantically called her office assistant to ask if she would go to her office and look through her personal files to find a copy. All the while, she also checked her computer and email for any sign of it. She, then, reached out to a church friend to ask if she knew of anyone from the church office who could look in their files with the slightest of hope that they might have a copy. She took another chance and called the hospital in Florida where my niece was born, but their patient information office was closed for the weekend. With all of her efforts, a copy was never found.

Nevertheless, there was still hope. I felt it. There was no way God would have brought her this far just to deliver disappointment. I even found myself standing in front of my recently departed mother's picture saying, "Do something about this!". Then, the storm turned into a drizzle. The church friend informed my BFM that she knew the Superintendent of my niece's school and that she was going to call him to see if they couwld get a copy from the school records.

A little glimmer of sunshine was becoming apparent when the Superintendent was able to contact my niece's school counsellor, and they were able to get into the school…on a Saturday morning…in the middle of summer vacation and obtain a copy of the birth certificate.

By 10:00am, she had finally received the birth certificate by email after hours of panicked phones and endless computer file searches.

The rain had stopped, and the rainbow was out for everyone to see, but the waterworks didn't stop there. My BFM let her healing tears flow down her face with gratitude in her heart for those who came to her aide that very early Saturday morning. Out of that gratitude, she gave many thanks and thoughtful gift certificates to those who made the impossible possible.

At the end of the next eight days together, she and my niece had an amazing vacation that was 17 years in the making. So, no matter what the rain looks like and if God brings you this far, He does promise a rainbow.

What has your rain looked like that has been followed by a beautiful rainbow?

#2

<u>When in doubt, Be yourself</u>

As I have mentioned, my life took a turn after I was told I had cancer. During my recoveries, I got to examine my roles as a wife, a mother, a sister, a daughter, and a friend. All these hats I proudly wear. Although, I admit that I only like to wear them one at a time.

Who was I, now, that I had 'hung up my lab coat'? Better yet, who did I want to be? I have had this great opportunity to 're-invent' myself. What bits do I want to keep? What bits do I need to retire with my 'old' self? Now, that my body had been transformed, how about me!

<u>Me as a Wife?</u> I decided that the silly crap that runs through my head just needs to jump out of my mouth. I like to think I am funny, and my husband needs to know that cancer didn't take my sense of humor with it. In fact, it made me funnier. And thinking back on this year of 2017, he admits to laughing more at and with me than he ever has in our 19 years together. Good time, Good times!

<u>Me as a Mom?</u> My kids are so awesome! I have loved seeing them grow into young adults since they came from my body. They make me laugh, they make me proud, and they make me question and contemplate the evil that exists just outside of our front door. I want them to know from my mouth what is out there in the world. Not just the bad stuff, but the good things too. Beautiful things, peaceful things. To be open-minded and respectful of others even though there may be

a chance that it might not be reciprocated. To hear the truth from my experiences whether it be good, bad, and ugly.

<u>Me as a Sister?</u> I like to say that I have four sisters: my beloved and revered older sister, Holli, my unofficially adopted sister, Bev (aka D3), my sister-in-law, Micha, and my sister-from-another-mister, Carrie. And in turn, I am their sister. Holli and I have an identical tattoo of the cross with the word S-I-S-T-E-R-S across it. My relationship with them makes me a better version of Me because they are my sisterhood.

<u>Me as a Daughter?</u> When my mom passed, my sister and I are never too far from our dad. She lives across the street from him and I am only 7 miles from them. He has dinner with her most nights, but when it comes to doctor's appointments and hospital visits, that's my department. Nobody could ask for a better Daddy. He is also an amazing and loving grandfather to all his grandkids. I feel honored to be his and mom's daughter. I thank God for letting them be my parents.

<u>Me as a Friend?</u> I am very fortunate to be able to count past my fingers and toes of the fun and supportive friends of my inner circle. I dare not name anyone out of fear of leaving somebody out, but YOU know who YOU are! I trust God 100% with whoever He brings into my life. I can say that most of my friends are very diverse. I learn so much from them that I almost consider myself to be well-rounded just being in their presence. I would like to thank these dear friends for helping me stay positive and open-minded to the beauty of humanity. Love All Ya'LL!

<u>Me as Me?</u> I recognize that my personal strengths are being very organized and creative, but my weaknesses are not being able to fix my own hair and being affectionate towards others. But this year, I want to be so far out of my comfort zone that I won't remember where I started or where I might end. I have even let go of planning anything. If it happens, great! If it doesn't, it wasn't meant to be. Onto the next thing!

It is never too late to reinvent 'yourself'. It helps to start with a Pros and Cons list that "YOU" make on a piece of paper in blue pen. Nobody else. Even ask God to reveal your hidden strengths and give you courage to overcome those 'not so fond of' characteristics. He might be the best One to ask since He already knows you and loves you.

What is your view of You, not someone else's?

#3

A distant relationship is beginning to look more promising

The one word that stands out in this fortune is 'distant' which means "having a great amount of separation between each other'. To go a little further, the word 'separation' brings up a negative feeling of which I am not a fan. Which brings up the question: Separation from Who or What?

I am physically separated from my mom who passed away three years ago, but I feel closer to her now that she is with God than I did when she was here on Earth. I know that she is still with me every day. I feel separated from my beloved co-workers from all my laboratory jobs since I decided to stay home with my children, but I am only a text and Facebook post away from catching up with them. However, there is one relationship that has been 'distant' but is 'looking more promising' and that is with my husband. Confused? Let me es-plain!

This year of 2017, my husband and I celebrated our 19th year of marriage. In this same year, our two children have matured past the "hands-on", day-to-day grooming from when they were much smaller. Our daughter and son are in high school and middle school, so their days are busy with schoolwork, extracurricular activities, and friends. I believe they are handling their independent beginnings (but still heavily monitored by us) with respect and integrity. This leaves a lot of time for each other. We have had many dinners where we have addressed the question of the upcoming and impending Empty Nest Syndrome. We have even started a list which currently contains:

- I go back to work full-time. I have been keeping up my yearly dues and continuing education for my med tech certification. Most likely, I will work in a hospital lab on a set schedule. I thrive on a routine.
- After our son and daughter are registered and settled into their colleges, we are going to the airport (with our passports, of course) and take the next plane out to 'anywhere but here' for two weeks. We can buy clothes when we get to our destination.
- We put the house on Air B&B and set out in our RV to visit all the national parks in America.

This list is only in its beginning stages. Remember, we have only been married for 19 years. The first five years, we didn't have kids, so we finished college, established careers, and created a home. When we did start a family, our roles as spouses and even friends changed dramatically because when you bring another human being into this world, those first five to seven years are a fight to the death for your own sanity let alone the survival of the next generation. Sometimes, the marriage is put on hold, and sometimes, spouses become enemies because there are only enough hours in the day to have a full-time job, care for small kids, cook dinner, and keep the house from falling apart. No marriage is without challenges, but you have to communicate. Just a sincere 'I love you and I am still committed to US!" can speak so loudly.

When he is stressed, and his hair is standing on end, I say these words, and his facial expression relays to me that he knows he is not alone. I have even been on the other side of this phrase when my menopause has set in, and I have lost my mind for a few days. He lets me have my say, then he repeats back to me, "I love you, and I love us."

We all need somebody. We are not designed to be alone. It does not matter if you are hetero, gay, or lesbian. We all need somebody that is kind to us and cares for us physically, mentally, and emotionally while we are hear on this Earth.

You hear of those couples that divorce after their kids leave the nest. It is a tale as old as time. But during our dinners, we have re-established the "Why' and the "What" of what we love about each other and even the new talents and personality traits we have acquired from being parents.

So, I am here to say to those who are knee-deep in baby/toddler/elementary school stages that you will survive. There is a light at the end of the tunnel, but don't forget to strap in your spouse when the roller coaster of parenting gets CRAZY. We all want to get off the ride in one piece.

What is a distant relationship that you wish was closer?

#4

Success is a journey, not a destination

I have it...The key to success! Want to hear it? I am ready to share it.

The Key to Success is **Individualism!**

That's right...be yourself. This is no secret, and we have heard this advice for decades. Only you can be you. I am the only me. My body, my mind, and my spirit were uniquely made by God Himself. Your body, your mind, and your spirit were uniquely made by God. And because God created us to share the 'present' with Him, he also created Jesus with his own mind, body, and spirit. Jesus knew his own individualism was Divine but separate from God, his Father...Our Father. His individualism centered around Love...the purest form of Love...God's Love. With this Love, Jesus told us... in person...here on this earth... that God loves us, and God wants us to love Him and others. Then, with this individualism, Jesus showed us His love...for us...by dying a horrible death through crucifixion. Not suicide, not poisoning, not even being stoned...crucified...public crucifixion. The documentation of these times about his death is overwhelming. So much so that our calendars and significant historical events are either labeled A.D. (After Death) or B.C. (Before Christ). Danggg! Most have been pretty important! Jesus could have fled, but he didn't. He could have pleaded or lied to Pontus Pilot, but he didn't. He knew who He was, and he used his individualism to change the course of humanity. Again…Dang!

August 29th, 2017, Hurricane Harvey flooded and devastated Houston, Texas and it's surrounding areas. During the days of the storm, neighbor was helping neighbor, rival was helping rival, and people were coming to together to save lives. Boats, churches, and convention centers in the south were full of those who had lost everything.

Meanwhile in the Dallas/ Fort Worth Area, a tiny mention of a gasoline shortage was put on social media. This tiny mention went viral, and it seemed that every man was for themselves racing to the gas pumps. Drivers waiting in lines for up to two hours just to fill up their tanks. Some wasted their own gas to sit in these lines. Store owners were placing plastic bags on the nozzles to show that the gas was gone. That lead others to seek gas elsewhere, but guess what? They had to use their gas to find the gas. Uh, something is not adding up! As I watched the mayhem unfold on the news, all I kept saying to myself was 'What a bunch of Sheep!'. Sheep just graze and follow their shepherd. In this case, the shepherd was a social media post to propagate Armageddon, and it was successful.

Spiritual warfare has a new battleground, and it is social media. The battle can 'rage' on by having the ability to reach every 7.5 billion souls on this planet. The Good, the Bad, and those caught in between tend to bring their influences through the internet.

Now, since God created our mind, our body, and our spirit, he also gave us another important gift…Free Will. Free Will to make our own choices. Free Will to be curious about our environment and to use our five physical senses and yes…our 6th sense that connects us directly to Him. We were all created with strengths and weaknesses. Not to be blindly led like sheep. Sheep don't have the ability to use their touch or even have good eyesight, thus the statement 'blindly lead'. They can't make their own choices. No Free Will like us. They have to be looked after. They don't even have the abilities to be successful or contribute to their community. Are you a Sheep?

Let's break from the herd, open our eyes and ears, reach out with our hands, and use our words to help others 'break free' and find their

God-given talents to progress forward humanity. Use your 6th sense to connect with God to understand what real love can do for you and your family. The Black sheep of the Family is being redefined as a Good thing.

God is Love, and He made us in His 'mirror' image. What do mirrors do? They reflect. God shines with love, we reflect it, and it bounces off others to create an amazing light.

However, negativity has a way of 'throwing mud' on our mirrors so nothing can be reflected, and our senses become dulled. This is probably why God likes to bathe us in water as to 'wash' off the mud. Just a little dip, and we are so sparkly. Others may need a few more dips or even a sandblasting to get the mud off, but guess what? Love is patient…and Love is kind!

It has to be your decision, your Free Will to find your individual freedom. Call on Jesus. He has been there, and He has done that. He didn't give his life to just sit on the right hand of God. He died to 'lead' you by the right hand to break from the herd.

Individualism is the key to your success because it is on your terms that you set with the help of God, not the public. Happiness and Peace are found within by your Free Will and your 6th sense, not social media or fake news. That stuff gets crazy real quick due to the simple concept of 'every man for themselves'. Don't be a sheep. We already have enough of those.

How will you break from the herd of the world?

#5

Be willing to assert yourself in situations of great importance

A very famous tune by the Beastie Boys "You have to fight for your right to party" comes to mind as well as "There is nothing like a Catholic party…because a Catholic party don't stop, don't stop!" Nevertheless, most Catholics are pumped up on wine and the Holy Spirit…present party included. But this outcome isn't about the party…It's about the Fight! The 'being willing to assert yourself in situations of great importance' for anyone and any cause that cannot or will not defend themselves.

For example, September 11th, 2001, those passengers on Flight 93 who knew their outcome wasn't going to be in their favor after the hijackers took over the plane. They fought back against their enemy to save the lives of many. The wife of passenger, Tom Beamer, coined the phrase "Let's Roll" after his and others decision to 'assert themselves in a situation of great importance'. Apparently, those brave men and women **did not** negotiate with terrorists, and it is in no question in my mind that they are with God who has made them into Guardian Angels for their families who they left here on earth.

My natural instincts when faced with a confrontation is more flight than fight, but something changed this year of 2018. God has pointed out that it is time to start taking up for myself, my kids, and my marriage. This year, I am calling the devil out on his lies. In the forefront of my mind, Jesus and I are looking at each other, and I say to Him, "Let's Roll!". The devil is the ultimate terrorist, and I am strong enough now with the ever-loving presence of My Savior to call him out on his lies because Jesus is the Truth. I want to extend that strength to my husband in our marriage and to my children while they are still under my roof and impressionable. I want us as a family to practice putting on the full 'Amour' of the Lord to help protect ourselves from evil.

Did you notice that the word "amour" in languages like Spanish, French, and Italian translate to the English word "Love"? So, the 'Amour' of the Lord is also the "Love" of the Lord!

So, when I need to 'assert myself in any situation of great importance', I will be doing it with the Love and Truth of the Lord because every situation is another opportunity to share my faith and 'fight the good fight' to keep peace and joy in my life.

How are you fighting the 'Good Fight'?

#6

Your warmth radiates upon those around you

The more I write about the events that I think have made me a stronger, the more inquisitive I have become with my friends about their stories of triumph over hardships. These curious observations have been extended to those around me, especially pertaining to one stranger I met in an airport that definitely gets my vote for a Tough Cookie Award.

In the summer of 2018, I had my ticket to go see my sister-from-another-mister, Carrie B, who lives in New York State. The reason for the trip was to see her, but it was also to help her travel from NY to her hometown in Oklahoma via Dallas with her three young children. With the kids out of school and a lighter work schedule, an opportunity presented itself to her to make plans to visit her parents who are half a country away.

My bestie, Carrie, is married, and her husband is probably one of the most interesting guys I have ever met. In fact, Carrie and I had a great NYC weekend just so I could meet him before they started getting serious. My nickname for him is Mr. New York City. He has his Juris Doctorate, but his passion is politics. After meeting him and getting an amazing, historical commentary tour of New York City, I put my stamp of approval on him. Currently, Mr. NYC is in the throes of his own political race. This is why he was unable to travel with Carrie to Oklahoma with their family.

After informing me of her dilemma to come see her family, I told her that I would fly up there and fly back with her and her tiny crew. She said, 'Are you sure?' Then, I reminded her of the time that she got that job in New York State, and I flew out to North Carolina to drive her car with her dog while she drove her dad's truck which was full of her personal belongings along with her dad that was driving the U-Haul to move her north into the next chapter of her life. When you are friends with me, there are serious benefits ☺.

We took the next few days to check availability and prices of the most popular airlines and plotted our course. I had a one-way ticket there, and then she added me to their itinerary back to Dallas where her mom and dad would pick them up. Since I was only going to be home the next day, I lightly packed a backpack with a change of clothes and toiletries. I hardly ever travel by myself and never as light as this, but it was a nice change to not have to check a bag.

I arrived early at the airport as anyone should nowadays and passed uneventfully through security. I stopped at an airport convenient store for a bottle of water and some snack then sat down to wait for boarding. So simple, so laid back, so freeing to just have a small carry-on. However, this was not the situation for the stranger I was about to meet.

While I was waiting for my boarding group to be called, a little dark-haired girl came and sat in the chair beside me. I looked up from the book I was reading to make eye contact with her and gave her a smile. Behind her, I saw a young mother carrying a baby in her arms and two carry-on bags. I looked back at the little girl to see that she too had a backpack with her. Then, another woman came up to the young mother with a car seat that had another baby strapped inside. She sat the carrier down and told the young mother to have a nice flight. This young mother was by herself with twins around the age of 6-9 months old and a little girl about 6 years old. All I could think about was 'Did she have to park, or did someone drop them off? How did she get through the ticket counter and security? And, how is she going to get on that plane?'

I sat there very patiently and quietly waiting to see if anyone was going to offer to help her onto the plane. The flight attendants started to call the boarding groups. One by one, the passengers lined up and proceeded along their journey. Nobody saw this young mother to ask if she needed any help. Not even those who were sitting next to us who were obviously watching every move she made and listening to every cry of the baby she was holding.

Leave it to my inner voice to start yelling at me at this point. It said, "Hey, ask her if she needs help. You know she needs it. Do it." So, I did, and I saw relief and peace smooth over her face. She thanked me for offering, and we looked on her tickets to check which row and seats would be their resting place for the next three hours. She was on row 17, and I had row 28 on the same side of the plane.

Our boarding group number was being called, and I threw on my small backpack, grabbed the carrier with baby number one, and one of her carry-ons. She went ahead of me with baby number two, and the little girl was in between. We got all checked in and headed down the gangway with everyone and everything in tow.

Inside the plane, it was very cramped with passengers and their luggage. All trying to find their spots. She found her row, and the little girl got into the window seat and buckled herself in. The young mother held baby number two in one hand and stuffed her bag into the overhead bin with the other. As I was making my way to her row, a young gentleman was making his way back towards us to find a place for his bag. We stood head to head at row 12. He was looking at me, and I was looking at him. I piped up to break the tension, "Seriously, Dude? I have a baby…in a carrier." Then, that ass hat started to move pass me. I had to lift the baby carrier up over the heads of the passengers in row 12 as if presenting the baby to the plane like Simba in the Lion King. At that moment, I let the thought of punching him in the throat dance around in my mind, then I told it to move on because I didn't want to take a risk of getting thrown off. That would not help anyone. Nevertheless, we made our way to row 17, and she buckled the carrier into the middle seat. I made my way to the back of the plane and found my seat.

Three hours later and a very crazy landing, we were in NY and beginning our disembarkment from the plane. I peeked over the seats to quickly make eye contact with the little girl. I gave her a wave, and she gave me a smile with two thumbs up. I mouthed to her to wait for me, and she answered with a nod of her head. I can't start to tell you how much this little girl had stolen my heart. She was so helpful to her mom and was great at soothing her sisters. She was so kind, polite, and full of moxie when she was talking to me. I let her. I let her steal a piece of my heart.

Eventually, I made my way back to row 17 where I grabbed a bag and baby number two who was now in the carrier. As a well-oiled machine, we made our way off the airplane, through the terminal, and down to baggage claim. The young mother informed me that her sister was right outside and would be helping her the rest of the way. She thanked me and hugged me, and I hugged her back and wished her a safe flight back home. Then, the little girl thanked me and hugged me, and I told her that she was a wonderful big sister. Reluctantly, I left them there to find the sweet face of my bestie, Carrie B, who was picking me up and repeated the process with her the next day.

How is it that this very short and fast trip wielded a story of two tough cookies who happen to be traveling on their own with other tiny cookies? A story of dilemma, a story of courage, and a story of strength emerged when the pull of family was at stake. The scientist in me would love to take blood samples of the tough cookies I know to explore the possibilities of a gene being found. If so, it shall be called the Tough Cookie Gene.

Write about the Tough Cookies you see in your life.

#7

<u>Travel with an open heart and positive expectations</u>

I love to travel, and the summer of 2017 was showing a lot of promise. Already planned for the month of June, our new Boy Scout, was going off to camp for the first time for a week, and our daughter was going to Oklahoma to stay with a beloved cousin for that same week. Then, my husband decided to take off that entire week of work as well. Hot Diggity-Dog! We were going to have a whole week just to ourselves. How was that going to work?! Don't worry, I have a plan for that ☺.

We love to cook together. He has been busy with work, so we don't get to do this often, so a night of wine, music, fresh veggies, and a juicy steak was on the menu for Monday. Tuesday was all about poolside. Another great time shared with sun, songs, and sodas, but these were just the appetizers.

My husband had been working on his instrument rating as a pilot for the smaller, single-prop planes. He has his private pilot's license, but the instrument ticket will let him fly in and around the clouds. He currently rents from a company at a nearby small airport. He had mentioned that he wanted to fly me somewhere special for our week together. He did a search and found the Hanger Hotel in Fredericksburg, TX.

This hotel is an actual hanger that has been converted. It sits just off the runway in Fredericksburg. You can even park your plane outside the front door. Convenient, huh! Sounds like a great time to be had!

At the time of our trip, he could only fly 'visually' which means no clouds and able to see the ground. Unfortunately, the Texas early summer was ever rainy and cloudy. He had established a 'No-Go' criteria before he ever started flying, and he was watching the weather hourly the morning of our flight. By mid-morning on that Wednesday, there were clouds coming up from Houston and the air was really warm which could cause a little bit of turbulence. So, he pulled the plug on the flight. Oh Man! Super Sad Face ☹. Well, I still wanted to go. I wanted to get out of the city and out of the house for a new perspective and some relaxation. So, I told him that I would drive the 5 hours it would take us to get to Fredericksburg. Yeah, it was only going to be a two hours plane ride. What a bust! But, I have an open-mind and was holding on to my positive expectations for the remainder of the week. Boom!

Normally when we go anywhere, he does the driving, but he was in need of a vacation as well this week too. So, I plotted my course.

The drive was long, but beautiful. Hwy 281 is a two-lane paved road through the Texas Hill Country. Small towns and farms paint the scenery for an amazing and relaxing drive. Don't worry, there are gas stations and local cafes along the way. So, we took our time.

We quickly found The Hanger Hotel, parked the car, and headed towards the entrance. Right past the entrance, there was a porch with rocking chairs and the runway. They encouraged you to have a seat and watch the planes come in. All that was missing was a cooler of cold ones!

We went inside to check into our room. The lobby and downstairs was decorated in 1940s aviation. So cool! All the rooms where located up the spiral staircase just to the right of the front desk. We settled in our room and went down for dinner. The hotel had another hanger just next door that was converted to a diner, but they only served breakfast and lunch. So, we headed back to the downtown area to find a place to eat. The only place open was the Silver Creek Beer Garden and Grill. The patio was shaded and there was live music from a local guitarist. We ate, drank, and enjoyed not moving for a little bit.

We headed back to the hotel with a full belly, then my husband saw a sign in the lobby for an Officer's Club. No harm having a night cap to continue our wind down.

Across from the front desk was a set of glass doors that where open to their fullest. Inside was an amazing room with a beautiful fireplace and four red suede rolling chairs around it. I was already feeling cozy from the apple cider beer from dinner, but I was even more comforted by my surroundings.

Off to the left, there was another small gathering room with chairs, and to the right, there was a pool table, the bar, and another set of red, suede chairs around a small table. On that small table was the card game Card Against Humanities. I had seen it before, but never played it. We got a round of drinks and sat in the red chairs with the card game. Three other people were there in the club playing pool. I asked them if they wanted to play with us. They introduced themselves, and we started playing.

We proceeded to play Cards Against Humanity well into the late hours of the evening. I have only one thing to say about the game: It was so bad that it was THAT good. I laughed until I peeped myself a little. Best night of the year EVER!

About midnight, the bar was closing, and we headed back to our room for a good night's rest. Tomorrow, we would do breakfast, then head out to do some wine tasting. I was still going to drive home so the hubs could continue enjoying his relaxation.

The week spent together was great. We relaxed and enjoyed each other's company. None of 'we need to do this' or 'we need to do that'. Just straight takin' it easy. We didn't get to fly, but the view from the front seat was still amazing. I love to travel, and after this week, I will always travel with an open-heart and positive expectations for adventure because God has already set up his blessings for me along the path that He has chosen.

Happy Travel Blessings!

What has been your favorite trip or places to go?

#8

<u>Work on improving your exercise routine</u>

Let us start this fortune out with a huge eye roll, if not full body slump forward. I just cannot convey how much I hate to exercise, but you really do have to do it.

You really don't appreciate your hormones when you have them because you are too busy hating them. Your monthly cycle, the tender boobs, the bloating of the abdomen, and the random irrational emotions and outbursts are just a few symptoms of the fluctuating hormone levels that nature deems necessary to propagate the species…until something goes wrong, and you have to get your ovaries taken out which means… you in menopause, bitch!

However, these hormones are just as important for reproduction but are needed to sustain the female body for longevity. Let's have a little science lesson on Estrogen:

The term 'hormones' are chemical messengers that carry information from one group of cells to another. Therefore, 'hormones' influence almost every cell, organ, and function which includes our growth, development, metabolism (this is the important one for weight loss), tissue function, sexual function, the way our bodies use food, and how the body reacts to an emergency.

Estrogen circulates in the bloodstream and binds to estrogen receptors on all cells such as the brain, bone, liver, heart, and other tissues such as connective tissue like skin.

According to a study from the National Cancer Institute in 2002, regular exercise can cause a significant decrease in estrogen levels and can contribute to a lowering the risk of getting breast cancer. You see this commonly with athletes such as gymnasts and ballet dancers who do not get their cycles until later in their teenage years.

Now that I have this information, I need to apply it to my new estrogen-free life style to keep everything working properly. If gymnastic and ballerinas can be lean, strong, and fabulous with low estrogen levels, then exercise is a MUST!

So, what kind of exercise will you do, Jill? So, glad that you asked.

Cycling either in a studio or on the road, cross-fit, and Zumba are the hottest types of workouts nowadays, but do I want my body to do that? My brain says, 'Jill, me and the body have been talking, and it doesn't want to do any of those things. No thank you and drive thru.' But what my body did tell my brain was, 'Suggest yoga to her.'

Lol, I love yoga! You can strengthen and build muscle, which is a great support for your bones, plus burn calories and increase flexibility. Everything your body needs in a cooled and peaceful environment. With soft music playing in the background, the ability to be fully clothed, and the scent of refreshing essential oils should have anybody ready to say, 'Sign Me Up!' So, I try to yoga once or twice a week, but I love to walk my dog, Maggie Mae, every day. Great for me, great for her, and seeing that neither one of us have our ovaries, the exercise has been kind to us.

How will you work to improve your exercise routine?

#9

The best angle from which to approach any problem is the 'TRY'-angle

Huge eye-roll! I think I know where this is going to go with this fortune…

We all have strengths and weaknesses. I love to organize, clear clutter, and garden. However, I HATE to cook. My mom was an amazing cook. She was a true Southern Woman, and she could whip up the most delicious biscuits and gravy from scratch at all hours of the day. Her lists of good country cooking were endless, and she never used a recipe.

My house is orderly, and my kitchen is clean, but the day to day tacks of planning, shopping, unloading and putting away those groceries, and cooking two meals, (three if you have little ones at home) a day for a busy family is…A Full-Time Job!

I can do laundry all day, every day. Even clean toilets and throw-up until the cows come home, but cooking has become almost like a Goundhog's Day full of Mondays. Ahgggg! Then came Emeals, Blue Apron, and Hello Fresh. Well, Hello helpful cooking ideas.

We started using these meal helpers about five years ago. It takes all the guess work out of feeding the family. You pay their fee, and every week you get seven meals with a detailed shopping list along with cooking instruction. You can even choose what kind of meals you want from Kid-Friendly, Clean Eating, Carb-Smart, Paleo, etc. We started out doing the Clean Eating menus but switched to Kid-Friendly when my husband and I were the only ones eating the dinners, and I was cooking the kids something separately.

The routine starts on Sunday when we print out our meals for the week. Over the last few years, we don't do well with pork, even with helpful cooking instructions, so we cross out those recipes. Then, we take an inventory of the refrigerator, freezer, and the pantry. You don't save money by buying two or three of everything, then we set off to the store.

The shopping list is organized by department. They say that the best way to buy the best food is to shop from the outside walls and not the isles. All of your healthier items should be found fresh or frozen and not canned or bagged. Of course, there are always exceptions. We start in the produce section first, then diary and cheese, onto meats, and end up running down a few of the isles. For a weeks' worth of meals (not really counting breakfast), we spend less than an hour shopping and an average of $160 to $200.

On the nights that we prepare our gatherings, I like to have some music playing in the background, and the hubs likes a little bit of white wine because red gives him a headache. The kids are close by 'hopefully' doing their homework ☺. By the end of our cooking escapades, the house smells great, bellies are full, and the family has had time to catch up with the day's transactions.

Using these meal helpers has been my TRY-angle for our cooking catastrophes, and it has helped me save time, money, and energy. The painful loop of cooking is painful no more.

What have been some of your cooking catastrophe stories?

#10

You will be changing your present line of work

Oh, Man! Here we go again!

When I read this fortune, I laugh out loud…a few times…and say. "Yeah, it's about that time again." The last job I had "outside of the home" I was there for five years which was a record for me. It wasn't that I couldn't keep a job. I just was presented with some fresher opportunities.

My very first job was working in the salad bar/ produce department at a grocery store. I was there full time during the summer then went part time once college started back. I gained a lot of work ethic with this one, and I was there for one year.

I decided that I needed something more in the medical field since that was what I was focusing on in college. I found a courier job for a pathology lab. It was a lot of fun, and I gained experience and knowledge of the human anatomy and how to drive a stick-shift. When I transferred to the local university from community college, I had to change my job due to my new schedule. I was there for two years.

One of my pathologists had a clinical laboratory that was mainly for outpatient lab work and a draw station. He told me to go talk to the supervisor and see what they had open. They did have an opening for a front desk clerk, and I took it. This was my first introduction to the profession of Medical Technologist. I was there for two years.

After I graduated from college, I had planned to continue on to a Physician's Assistant Program, but I was too burned out of the college life and was ready to earn some money. This led me to Baylor University Medical Center in downtown Dallas. Even though I only had a Bachelor's in Science, this job was doing actual med tech-ing. The department I was working in was called Transplant Immunology. We preformed tissue typing for kidney, heart, lung, and bone marrow transplants. We also preformed crossmatches for organ donors to ensure no rejection would occur for the patient. These crossmatches were done 24/7 so being on-call was part of the job. Some weeks you literally worked the night shift. When I was on-call and saw a motorcyclist speeding down the highway, I would say, "That idiot is going to get me called in tonight." Being on-call started to take its toll, so I followed a co-worker to another job that was closer to home, more pay, and NO CALL. I was at Baylor for a year and a half.

My next job was for Arlington Cancer Center in the Bone Marrow Processing Lab. We would harvest stem cells from patients, store them for cryogenics, and re-infuse them back into the patient to boost their immune system after they underwent high doses of chemotherapy. I was there for two years until my husband and I were transferred to Preston, England for six months. Opportunity of a Lifetime!

After our stay in England, I was pregnant with our first born, and I thought I would try staying at home. Two years later, I had a son, and then another two years after that, I was ready to go back to work. My babies had outgrown me and were ready for something more challenging. Our beloved next-door neighbor (aka RaRa) owned and operated a nearby childcare and learning center. I knew that my babies were being well cared for while I was away from them.

Knowing that I would one day return to work, I applied to take the Medical Technologist certification exam through the American Medical Technologists certifying organization. I had my Bachelor of Science and three years of experience as a med tech and was accepted to sit for the exam. Best Decision I ever made! After passing the exam, I was free to move about the laboratories.

My first job back to work was back at the Baylor Transplant Immunology lab…again. I had reached out to a mutual friend, and she said that they were hiring. I was back here for three years until that other famous co-worker called to ask me to come back to Arlington Cancer Center again because they needed my skill set. Well, my skill set was mostly being organized, pleasant, efficient, and able to write some awesome Stand Operating Procedures (SOPs).

Back at Arlington Cancer Center, this job wasn't in the bone marrow lab, but the general main lab. I love new challenges, and I absolutely loved this job. I learned to draw blood, troubleshoot instruments, and fix technology. Every day was an endless learning experience. I loved to draw blood and meet my patients every chance I got. In a cancer clinic, you see your patients a lot, and you form relationships. You bond with the families, and when a loss occurs, you feel it too. I loved holding, feeding, and playing with my babies, but I also loved being with my mom as she left this world one late April evening. She had died of lung cancer, and I was fortunate enough to be able to be with her during treatments and doctor visits since she was being treated at my work. I knew she was going to Heaven to be with God, but I know she is always with me now. I was there for five years.

After the loss of my mom, my husband and I talked about me staying home again. Another reason for this discussion was that our daughter was starting middle school, and we were not hearing the best of things from other parents. So, we decided that my focus needed to be more on the home front. Well, after two months of staying home, I was diagnosed with breast cancer. At least I knew where I would be going for treatment. This time I was on the other side of clinic door. It took four months and three surgeries to get rid of a dis-ease and what caused it. Stupid Ovaries! I decided to vote those bitches off the island, but unfortunately, they left with both my boobs. However, here is where is gets good…

In the winter of 2015, I was cancer-free and looking for something to do while the kids were back in school. I started a little side hustle called Straightened Up. It was me exercising my organizational skills. I organized one huge house and decided it wasn't for me. Going through someone else's stuff was physically and emotionally draining.

Then, in the winter of 2016, my sister and I started making all natural, olive oil soap. We called our little biz Olive-U-Clean.

This makes me think of that bible verse from Ecclesiastes 3: 1-8 "There is an appointed time for everything, and a time for every affair under the heavens…etc.", and like the fortune says, "I might be changing my line of work. ", but I say, "Bring it on!" I have proven that I can pick up what God wants to put down because "I am Spartacus!".

What would be your dream job?

#11

Investigate the new opportunity that will soon become an option

Who isn't a little leery of new opportunities?! I am not normally a skeptic, but somethings can be too good to be true.

So, I must ask myself…Is being a writer actually an option? Yeah, if you have a career already and want "a side hustle'.

I have found that it takes a lot of cash up front and several trips outside my comfort zone to self-publish a book. Just one book. Writing has been the easy part, but you also need to be disciplined enough to sit down with either a pad and pencil like Moi or at a computer to let the creative juices flow.

Editing is the natural next step. I enjoy doing my own editing. I have loved all my English classes from middle school all the way up into my college years. Editing somehow gives me a false sense of control over my current project ☺. But I suggest letting friends read and critique or pay to have it professionally edited. Then, off to the publishers where they format and print your latest creation.

Now about marketing, I tend to want to roll into the fetal position when I think of marketing in general. Naturally introverted and frugal with my money, I find the concept of 'spend money to make money' not quite efficient. But, here lies another question…will this book make money? This is where I take my hands off the wheel and engage God.

Only He knows the true plans for the book(s). For example, the book 'The Shack' by William Paul Young was professionally published in 2007, but he claims to have written it a few years before. The movie came out in 2017, and I heard good things about it. A friend of mine suggested I read the book first. So, I picked it up at my local bookstore and read it. Having been a believer in the Holy Trinity all my life, this book changed my perspective (for the better to clarify) of God's love and Jesus's purpose for dying for my sins. I did decide to see the movie with extremely high expectations. I loved the cast, and on some level, I hope that when I do see God that He looks and sounds like Octavia Spencer. I am particularly fond of her ☺. In retrospect, I found it interesting that I didn't need the book when it came out in 2007, but the impact that it did have on me in 2017 was more than just profound. I would like to think that my books will find those who need to read them when they need to be read.

I, also, prefer to write essay style because deep down I like to think I am funny, and it seems that everyone else is writing a novel. The whole month of November is dedicated to those writing a novel and helps to keep them motivated to finish it.

When my first book came out in 2017, I had already written the journal entries 15 years prior to re-editing, submitting, and the whole publication process. My observation of the process has already been mentioned in the start. So, with these observations and investigations, I have concluded that writing is a great option for me but seeing that it might be slim pickings for doing it full-time, I will hang on to my day job.

What book has made a difference in your life?

#12

<u>You will discover something fun from your investments this month</u>

The Merriam-Webster definition for an 'investment' is "an Outer Layer". Really Merriam-Webster…an outer layer?! No, do the hokie-pokie and turn yourself around…an Outer layer is what it is all about? Well, let us break down this "Outer Layer".

To the human body, our 'outer layer' is the skin. It protects the body from the environment and creates a prettier package than just looking at our innards. An 'outer layer' could constitute a shield or protection like Kevlar (aka bulletproof vests) for police officers or a lab coat and goggles for a scientist. These concepts are for our physical means, but what about your future? What about your hard-earned money?

Some people use the stock market. But after 1929, 1987, and 2008, I wouldn't be surprised if others have mattresses full of cash. Unfortunately, World War II brought us out of the Great Depression. After 1987, the Roth IRA became quite popular. Then in 2008, Americans were losing their homes to the banks which created a surge of house flippers. And just like writing a book, you have to write about 'what you know'.

When choosing stocks, look at the physical needs of your own life. What do you spend your money on most? Let me use myself as an example.

I start my day with a cup of coffee. I end my day with a few pips of chocolate. And in between, I like to make soap, organize my house, and garden. I currently have a Roth IRA. It is a great idea. Small savings over time does get bigger, but I also have stock in Hershey's and Home Depot. The world is never going to stop eating chocolate, and homeowners and trade professionals need tools and supplies on a whim. Nevertheless, chocolate, wood, recycled metals, and plants are renewable resources.

Try to contribute $20 or $50 a month to a savings account, but if you get some birthday or graduation money, invest in something fun that applies to your daily needs such as Starbucks, Lowes, Ace Hardware, Apple, or Microsoft, ect. You will be surprised by what the human race cannot live without.

Speaking of the human race, we are living longer. Even starting a savings account in your 40s can still be beneficial for you in the long run. To further prepare, create a will. You can just type something up on your computer and have it notarized. Just put it where you and another trusted individual will find it.

What are the daily things you invest in?

#13

Truth? You CAN handle the Truth!

I laughed so loud when I read this fortune. I almost choked on the piece of cookie that was already in my mouth.

The movie "A Few Good Men" is one of mine and my husband's favorite movies.

"You want me on that wall! You need me on that wall!" – Jack Nicolson

"Are we clear?" – Jack Nicolson

"Crystal!" - Tom Cruise

So, I ask you, "What are the 'Truths' you need to handle in your life at this moment?"

Not the ones from the past, it is time to let them go

Not the ones in the future, they do not even exist!

The ones you woke up this morning thinking about.

Could it be 'truths' about your job? your kids? your house? your unhealthy habits, or even about your significant others' unhealthy behaviors?

What is the one thing that you lie to yourself about?

Let us take today to tell ourselves the truth because… you CAN handle it!

Make a mental list and write it down. Then, think of solutions to the bad truths and praise the Lord for the good truths.

If there are some 'truths' that are overwhelming, I have found that a trusted counsellor can bring a different perspective and creative solutions to my difficult issues because sometimes, we cannot see the forest for the trees.

And in the year of 2018, one of my 'truths' was that I have self-worth as a stay home mom. The lives of my family would seize to exist unless I have not analyzed it, organized it, prepared for it, and executed it. As a woman, this is my superpower!

The three fundamentals of living are food, clothing, and shelter.

A man might have killed the food, but I prepare this food to feed my family.

A man may have grown and harvested the cotton and wool, but I have used my hands and skills to create a garment to cover and protect the blessed temples of my family.

A man might have used his physical strength to build the walls and construct a roof over our heads, but I light the fire in the fireplace to warm the inside, set the table to eat our meals, and dress the beds where we are to rest our mind and bodies.

The truth is…I am a woman whom God created out of the rib of a man, and I am worthy of the Love from My God and respect from every man.

"What say you?!"

What are your truths?

_____

_____

_____

_____

_____

_____

_____

_____

_____

_____

_____

_____

PEACE OF POETRY:
THE FORTUNE COOKIE

*There you are… my sweet, little confection
With your folded ends… pointing in my direction.
You beckon my attention… without making a sound.
I stare at you lovingly… even though others are around.
You are my cookie. I stake my claim on you.
Your mysterious message inside… better not be about food.
My belly is full of chicken and rice,
But don't you worry… I have plenty of room inside.
I reach for you slowly… imagining your taste.
There will not be a single morsel of you… that will ever go to waste.
You crack so easy…piece by piece.
The sound sends chills from my head… down to my feet.
From crunch to crunch…I confess that I love you too much.
That even my fortune expresses, "You will have a wonderful lunch."*

Fortune Cookie Contest

Feel free to crack open a fortune cookie, write me a story, and submit it to be featured in the next book 'Outcomes of a Fortune Cookie: Wise Cookies', and 6 will be the magic number.

You can submit your stories via my website at www.jillgandy.com and remember to include a thoughtful question at the end to prompt our reader's creativity.

#14

The Self-Proclaimed Fortune: The ability to talk to yourself is a well needed dialogue to put truth into perspective

Do you talk to yourself? Do family members ever ask you who you are talking to when you are in a room alone? Does your dog or cat tilt their head when you ask them a question because they know it is just you and them?

I love to talk to myself! I do it a lot. I do it in the shower, walking the dog, putting away the laundry, and cooking. And not just in my head…out loud. I have had my husband ask me who I am talking to, and I answer 'Me'. In a few of these essays, you can catch me writing in the third person and asking myself questions. I like to think I am funny, and I have "Random Thoughts of Silliness'. I will burst out laughing… in public when I am clearly alone. The mind is a terrible thing to waste, and when I am not with friends and family members sharing my time, I am with me.

Did you know that humans ARE three dimensional? There are actually seven dimensions of Creation:

1. Our Planet. The very Earth we live on.
2. Nature and Elements. Trees, Air, Water, Our Bodies and the processes that make it run.

3. The Human Mind and Self-Awareness
4. Our Spirit including Our Higher-Self
5. Unconditional Love and Unity with God and His Light (Heaven), plus Angels and Demons
6. The Void – Here lies all the secrets of the how the Universe works
7. God – Our Beloved Creator

We consist of the Second, Third, and Fourth dimensions, but it truly is the Third, Fourth, and Fifth that makes the difference in our human lives here in One and Two. So, when you open up conversations with yourself, you can also open up opportunities to have a dialogue with Jesus and with God himself. It is one of the concessions of Jesus dying for us on the cross, so we CAN have direct access to the Father. He does talk to us. We are just really bad at listening.

The best way for me to stay in contact with my beloved Creator and Jesus is being alone and reading from quick daily devotionals. It is as if He really is talking to me and reassuring me that He is always near, and I can call out to Him for good things and bad things.

As humans, we all pose the question, "How can you have a relationship with someone you can't see or feel?" And, this is where talking to yourself comes into play because that dialog that you are having with yourself is really from the Fourth and the Fifth. Just be warned: Negative conversations from Not-So-Nice spirit is always possible. This is how the devil works… to instill doubt of self and separation from others who love you. So always ask yourself, is this conversation pleasant, loving, and supportive verses depressing, hurtful, and selfish? And remember, we all have Free Will to decide to act upon the pleasant and loving thoughts as well as the hurtful and selfish ones.

Do you ever talk to yourself, and What do you say?

#15

<u>Your respect for others will be your ticket to success</u>

When I start my 'fortune rants', I like to resonate with at least one of the words in the fortune to help initiate a memory with a life lesson. The word 'respect' tends to tingle the hairs on the back of my neck for this one. I, then, go to Merriam-Webster.com to help simplify its meaning and correlate to the life lesson. According to Merriam-Webster, the word 'respect' is a relation or act of giving particular attention. So, I deduct that the relationships and acts of kindness I hold as important will be the catalyst for my success.

At the age of 43, I have found that my successes are on a small scale but just as important to the ones I 'give particular attention'. Here are a few:

Respect for my husband as my partner in this life. Equal to me with strengths in areas where I am weak, admired father to our children, and renown engineer in his field of work. I have never met anyone else quite like him. He is literally the Yang to my Yin to an uncanny degree. He teaches me lessons of forgiveness and grace that only a man can teach a woman (eye roll). But most of all, he is my committed half, and I look forward to growing old with him.

Respect for my children and my extended family because without them, I would have no guidance for some of my purposes, no reasons to function with my strengths, and no excitement for future plans spent with them.

Respect for my friends who push me to be the best I can be and challenge me to move outside my comfort zone such as Erin B., who invited me to go to Oklahoma City to a Harry Potter Yule ball dressed up as witches, then crash an Allstate Insurance Christmas party that was being held at our hotel. Good Times! Good Times!

Last but of course never least, my respect for my God who created me. Well, He, also, created all these other wonderful people and put them in my life to enjoy and learn valuable lessons. I know that there will be more friends to come and more lessons to learn, but He is Faithful, and He is kind, and He is Love. Faith, Hope, and Love are all a part of the recipe for building respect in every relationship that I 'give particular attention'.

Who do you 'respect' to make you a success of your own story? Make a list. Check it twice. Mark the ones who are naughty and nice. But, don't forget about yourself. Respect for yourself teaches you how to respect others, and that starts a cycle of bringing joy into your life. In turn, joy promotes love, and love propagates success of any size whether great or small.

Your list here.

#16

Past Inspirations and Experience will be Helpful in Your Job

I believe that the toughest job to have is being a parent. I was in no way prepared to face the overwhelming challenges of the day-to-day tasks of keeping another small human alive and well. It is trial by fire, and sometimes there is actual fire. The phrase 'Did that just happen?' plays like a broken record in my head. During the really crazy times, I look at my husband to confirm that the look on his face suggests the same question is also playing in his head. However, I have found that relating to my children takes a large portion of my mental compacity. To help myself save some energy, I revisit my own childhood as a coping mechanism. "What do kids like to do?" is a constant inquiry. "What did 'I' like to do?" shortly follows. The answers have been eating ice cream, going swimming and roller skating, and playing on the playground. Also, they love birthday parties, hanging out with friends, and watching movies.

My daughter is so full of life. She reads and writes short stories like me, but she is also an amazing artist. She loves to draw. She admits to using drawing to de-stress. She has taken up photography using her grandmother's 1980s Canon 400 speed camera. I laugh a little bit to myself when she drops off the actual roll of film to be developed, and they tell her that it will take up to 10 days to get her pictures back. The look of 'this is not instant gratification' crosses her face with a huge teenage eye roll. I like to believe that I will never have to buy art again. See, she is already saving me money. Although, I have thought about buying stock in Michael's Arts and Crafts along with Hobby Lobby.

My son is a very old soul. He is one of a kind. He doesn't enjoy participating in sports, but he loves his Boy Scouts. He is also quiet the conversationalist, and someday wants to be an attorney. He has perfected the art of leading the witness as I have learned over the years. When I see that look on his face, I say, "Cut to the chase. I am not playing twenty questions. I have to go to the grocery store and finish the laundry." Then, he gives me smile and spills the beans. I feel that he will 'Always Be Prepared".

When the kids started school, my husband and I sat down and divided up the subjects to play to our strengths. He is a mechanical engineer, so he gets most of the harder math questions. I am a microbiologist, reader, and writer. So, I get biology and language arts. We both can handle the broader subject of science. However, we have given history over to Google. We have proof that the above formula works for our clan. Assess your likes and dislikes to be a practical part of the family unit.

The important aspect of parenting is to know your Strengths and your Weaknesses. As I say this, let me drop this right here. We are all Divinely created for this time and this place here on Earth. We are supposed to be different. Our collective differences are what keep humanity moving forward. When you become a parent, you are moving the human race forward with the next generation. Visit your childhood and try remembering the awesome moments so you can share them with your offspring. They may not tell you right away that it made an impact on them, but you took the time and effort to plant the joy! For my family, we love to roller skate. For my 33rd birthday, I bought myself white, high-top, blue quad roller skates with crazy colored laces just like I had when I was five. However, they do not like to go out to the country and pick pecans. You win some, and you lose some.

Do you have a crazy kid story?

#17

You should enhance your feminine side at this time

You would think that my thoughts for this cookie message would be a no brainer, but they were not.

At my core being, I am not 'fancy' or 'girly'. From early childhood, I have had family and friends help me along the way in this area of which I lack.

My older sister, the fashion diva of the 80s, loved to dress me up like a doll and do my makeup and hair. My mom knew how to sew and mended cute outfits to fit me, and my mother-in-law, aka Mrs. Chanel, encouraged me to spend a little extra money for jewelry pieces I would last me forever.

All of these tips worked to my favor until I was 39 years of age and elected for a double mastectomy after a diagnosis of breast cancer. When all the surgeries were done, I could not have felt more less of a woman than I was before. My body's transformation was quite a blow to my God-given female identity, but I decided to take a positive approach to this 'change' in life and re-invent myself for a new and improved 'Jill Elizabeth Hughes Gandy, the 1st'.

Within this 're-invention', I wanted to add something for everything I thought I had lost, then add accordingly.

First, I decide to go for the 3D nipple tatoos to finish off the new 'girls' and cover the scars. The procedure took about an hour. She matched my skin color and took some measurements. There wasn't any pain because I had not had any feeling in those areas since the surgery. I just heard a lot of buzzing. After she was done, I could not believe my eyes. She handed me a small mirror to see for myself. It was as if nothing ever happened. Her needle was a magic wand that erased all the bad and left only the beauty. I could not wait to get home and flash my husband.

Second, with the girls finally finished, I wanted to grow out my hair and go permanently blonde. I needed a professional hairdresser that was close, cost effective, and gay. So, my sister introduced me to her guy, and I won't let anybody touch my hair but him. I look forward to making that appointment when my roots are longer than I like. I even dress up for the occasion with a nice outfit and do my makeup so I can walk out as a finished product to the world.

And third, I decided to find a brand of clothes that fit my new shape for both my bigger top and my bigger bottom. With my certain breast cancer type, I made the decision to have a complete hysterectomy since the problem started in my ovaries, and I had no further use for my womb. This decision forced me into early menopause, and I gained a little unwanted weight. Luckily, God sent me new friend who just happened to sell Cabi clothing. Cabi stands for Carol Anderson By Invitation. You can read all about my love of Cabi clothes on my blog at www.jillgandy.com. These clothes just scream my name and make me feel prettier than ever before. Sure, they are a little pricy at first, but they are no more expensive than department stores, and Cabi stylists always have Sample Parties from past seasons, and you can get really cute and comfy pieces for almost nothing.

Physically, I am one sex organ away from being asexual, but emotionally and spiritually, I am all woman and loving the new and improved me. So, if you ever come to any of my book launches or readings, I am the curvy, short, blonde girl wearing colorful Cabi clothing.

What is your 'feminine' side morphing into?

#18

Someone is speaking well of you

Why is it as kids when we go to our parent's house to visit, we greet them with hugs and hellos, then immediately head to the refrigerator to see what is inside? Are we expecting to see that mom or dad has cooked something special for our visit? Maybe a chicken and rice casserole, or a bowl of leftover spaghetti? Well, one of my many visits, I open those doors to find something very interesting inside my parent's frig that was completely unexpected.

After having my daughter, my dad decided to finally retire from being in finance for the past 35 years, and he and mom moved from their cozy college town to the big city to be closer to us, but mostly their new grandbaby. During their unpacking process into the new home, I took a break to make us a few turkey sandwiches. As I was reaching for the turkey on the middle shelf, I noticed some folders in one of the bottom drawers. I said, "Daddy, why are there folders in the frig and not your office cabinet?"

He replies, "Oh Baby, those are mine and your momma's funeral plans."

Um, what!?

Apparently, he and mom each had a blue booklet, and within these booklets, there were plenty of details of their final moments from casket colors to curtain calls of their favorite choruses. Well, it does take out the guess work of the grief-stricken loved ones which would reduce the stress on the entire family and the funeral home staff.

Now that these particular items were covered, what about the eulogy? What are your friends and family going to say since you are not here to hear their words? What legacy are your leaving behind?

Furthermore, a friend and I were on our way to a writer's meeting, and we decided to ride together. We were coming to the end of our writing and looking for advice for our next steps. On the car ride there, she asks me, "Why did you write this book?"

My first thought was that this question was deep, and I would need some time to figure out a good answer for myself. This is why, I love this woman! She asks me really difficult questions that I need to be asking myself to keep me progressing towards my goals. But what was my goal for this book? It had been a year since we started writing together as accountability partners. So, I told her that I needed time to reflect on it, and I would get back to her. Then, I turned to ask her the same question.

She replies, "To leave a legacy. To leave a piece of me to remain long after I am gone from this world."

Wow! Her response added more questions to my thinking instead of answering them, but at least, I have a focus.

What do I want to leave as a legacy? What do I want people to say about me at my funeral? Will someone 'speak well of me' when I am gone from this world?

These questions and more are the forefront of my writing, editing, and expanding into unchartered territories of personality traits I might be keeping suppressed. It is one thing to journal about the events that happen to you, but it is another to format them into a book manuscript to submit for publication for the everyone to see. But Valentina is always encouraging me to be as transparent as I can and dig deep to find those emotions in the events to help connect with the reader.

However, if I get any more transparent, I might fade away. Thank you for reading our stories!

What will people say at your funeral?

#19

Be willing to take advice as to give it.

Humanity is built on helping one another. Part of helping is giving advice such as a seasoned mom sharing her time-saving tips with a new mother or an experienced business owner leading freshly driven entrepreneurs on a road to success. But where is the line between giving the advice and taking the advice? Well, I have a cute story to share on that very question.

My sister is five years older than me, but my kids are seven years older than hers. When she was a teenager, she would do a lot of babysitting. She loves kids! However, I never babysat, but I love my kids because they are mine. The statement of 'it is different when it's your own' completely applies to me.

When my kids were younger, nobody advised me about all the hard work it takes to keep these miniature humans alive. It is mentally, physically, and emotionally challenging. But I found that this is only in the beginning. You start to figure out what works for you and your growing family.

My sister and I have a close relationship. When my husband and I moved from Oklahoma to Texas for our jobs, she also moved shortly after. Even now, we only live seven miles from each other. But we couldn't be more different. She is extremely articulate with her responses at a drop of a hat. I take a little longer to compose mine. She is more sentimental, and I throw almost everything away that doesn't have a current purpose to my daily function. However, we are both good with our money, which we get from our dad, and we put God and family ahead of everything else, which we got from Mom.

But when I started having babies about thirteen years ago, she would say, "Jill, you need to do this, or Jill, you need to do that." I respected her advice since she had experience with babies from her babysitting days. But like I said, you start to figure out what works for your family.

Out of respect for her, I would respond with, "I will work on that." Then I would give her a quick smile and a single eyebrow raise. It's what you do when you want to show kindness on three to four hours of sleep.

Now that she had little ones, I say, "Holli, try this" because I have had positive outcomes with certain techniques. I soon see the light bulb go off in her facial expressions, and then the eyebrow goes up. She quickly says, "I will work on that" because that is what you say when you are going on four hours of sleep, constant laundry, planning meals for h-angry kids, and no shower for two days.

Like I have said previously, being a parent is a tough job, but it takes a village to raise up the next generation. So, be willing to take the advice as well as to give it.

P.S. This is one of our most famous inside jokes that is expressed with a single eyebrow raise. Lol!

What advice have you taken that has worked out to your benefit? Share your secrets.

#20

Your Love Life will be Happy and Harmonious

Crap, I hope so! The other alternative can be a little depressing and not exactly what I have been working towards. Yes, I said 'working'. Every relationship is work! Not just with a significant other or inside a marriage, but raising kids to be decent and loving adults, or spending time with friends takes a lot of energy, effort, and commitment. Sometimes, you need to commit to putting out the effort, then budget your energy to give each relationship that special light that only you possess. The more effort you give, the more intimate the relationship becomes. I use the word 'intimate' not for sexual reason because For the Love of Chocolate, not everything is sexual. The more intimate or close the relationship draws, the less energy is needed to sustain it. In fact, intimacy is the measure of effort flowing between two individuals that can create its own energy. Did you know that the Love between God and Jesus is so strong that it flows as the Holy Spirit to each and every one of us? Even you there in the corner thinking of mean things about your significate other and co-workers…God loves you too, and He doesn't want you to harm others or yourself. Just remember that as those negative thoughts make their way into your brain that you acknowledge them, then tell them thank you and drive through.

In 2015, some statistics showed that 1 out of 5 Americans are lonely according to the Huffington Post. You would think that with all humanities love of social media, that loneliness wouldn't even exist. Huh!

March 22, 2017, Fortune magazine released an article entitled "Chronic Loneliness Is a Modern-Day Epidemic" by Laura Entis. She starts her piece saying, "Humans were not designed to be solitary creatures. We evolved to survive in tribes. The need to interact is deeply ingrained in our genetic code." She goes on to quote John Cascioppo saying, "the absence of social connection triggers the same primal alarm bells as hunger, thirst, and physical pain." Have you ever noticed that when people get together, they eat, drink, and become merry? I love the commercial that came out the Fall of 2016. It was a young girl and her mother cooking Thanksgiving dinner in their very small apartment. The young girl would go out to their hallway and knock on the neighbors' doors. The neighbors would come out and bring their small table to add to others so that the tables lined up along the hallway. They also brought a side of something to eat for the table. As the table and neighbors reached the end of the hall, the young girl knocked on the last apartment door at the far end, and an older gentleman with a big grumpy frown opens it. She invites him to eat with them, and they live happily ever after. In a world with 7 billion people, there should not be loneliness. Sometimes, you have to be the one to make the commitment to give the effort as an example to others. Maybe they don't know or were not taught by their parents to make commitments to another person, or they might have been hurt. Somehow, I have a feeling that you have enough 'Light' inside you that can shine for the both of you until the other can see the light for themselves.

What ideas do you have for a relationship to be happy and harmonious?

_____
_____
_____
_____
_____
_____
_____
_____
_____
_____
_____
_____
_____
_____

#21

Something on four wheels will soon be a fun investment for you

This fortune is telling the truth, and here is why I know it to be true… Let's Go RVing!

My husband had stopped working 'for the man' in 2007 and opened up his own business. He is brilliant and honest, and God had amazing plans for him and the rest of the Dallas/ Fort Worth area. He was either on the road go to a job or at home writing reports. To this day, he doesn't have an office outside of the home to go to everyday which made him feel even more confined than working in a cubicle. By the end of 2007, his business was growing, and I had gone back to work full-time as well. Since we both were busy, we were looking for fun things to do as a family. So, we started looking at RVs since our neighbors had really enjoyed using theirs.

My husband has always had a truck, which I believe every busy family should have one, and he was looking to upgrade his ride to something with a towing package. I think we took a few weekends to looking at different RV brands, and which model would better suit our needs as a small family. We decided to go with a 5th-wheel, which is a travel trailer that hooks to the inside of the bed of the truck instead of the bumper hitch. We went with this method to reduce the 'sway' factor since this was our very first trailer.

Living in the very south of the DFW metroplex, we were close to Joe Pool Lake which was surrounded by two beautiful state parks, Cedar Hill and Lynn Creek. Before doing any camping, we laid down some criteria for any optimal camping experiences:

- Never go out on a holiday weekend! Too many drunks.
- Never go for just one night! Set up and tear down with two small kids doesn't add up.
- Never in the heat of the Summer! Unless we are traveling to somewhere cooler like Colorado. I don't sweat nicely.

Our very first campout was in our driveway. We took a whole week to pack it with little goodies. It was like moving into a really small apartment that was already furnished. There was a queen bed at the front, the kitchen and dining where in the middle, and the bathroom and bunk beds were in the rear. The beds even had mattress warmers that your turn on if were to get super cold. We had so much fun on our special camping weekends, but when we needed to move closer into the city for better driving convenience for our jobs, we sold our beloved trailer to another wonderful family with three boys. Oh Lort!

A few years went by, and my husband was still working from the house and having seller's remorse for our beloved mobile apartment. So, off the to the RV shows we went for the latest and greatest models.

The kids were older now and riding bikes, so we decided on a bumper pull travel trailer, so we could store and carry the bikes in the back of the truck. We looked at all the brands, but we still loved the Rockwoods. We ended up purchasing a 35-foot travel trailer, which was a little bigger than our other one. It had two entries, an island in the kitchen, a super sofa instead of a dinette/ love seat combo, and four bunk beds in the rear. After a few campouts, we concluded that bigger was not better and traded it in on our current trailer which we named Suzie Pothole! Yes, we love this trailer so much, she has a name thanks to our daughter! She is another Rockwood bunkhouse, but only 27-feet long and only one slide.

In the summer of 2015, we took Suzie and the family on a grand two-week adventure. Amarillo, TX to Albuquerque, NM to see some very missed friends and their family, then to Sante Fe, NM and on to Alamosa, Co where we stayed at the Great Sands Dunes National Park. Our primary destination was Sugar Loafin' Campgrounds in Leadville, CO which was located at 11,000 feet above sea level. We stayed there for five days. It was nothing short of magical! We hiked, biked, and river rafted to our hearts content. All the while, Suzie was waiting for us to return home for a shower, dinner, and comfy place to sleep.

On our way back home, we camped at the Garden of the Gods RV Park in Colorado Springs, CO. This place was beautiful, and the pool was heated…in the middle of July! The hubs did some biking through the gardens, and we visited the Air Force Academy. We reluctantly left Colorado to stay in Raton, NM, then back to Amarillo, TX, and made it back home. This trip brought us all together as a family, and we continue to camp locally every Thanksgiving since the kids have the entire week off from school.

So, if it has been on your mind to go RVing, go to some shows, but first assess what your family really needs before considering the option to buy or rent. It's a great way to get away, because you have can have a lake house on every lake in the beautiful US of A!

What 4-wheel adventure do you ever think about having?

#22

A pet will grace your presence

Have you ever heard of the phrase 'fish and family go bad in three days.'? Well, this also applies to my beloved, ADHD dog named Maggie.

She is a rescue I accidentally (wink, wink) stole from a heroin addict in the winter of 2014. She is a sweet and beautiful 5-year old golden border collie with a long, bushy tail. I love dogs with a tail. It is as if they have a built-in happy meter. However, on one particular morning as the sun was just poking up over the eastern horizon, a series of unfortunate events led to a very stinky ending.

I had just "stumbled into the kitchen and poured myself a cup of ambition" while my favorite Dolly Parton song was playing loudly in my head. Our kitchen faces the back of the house, and behind our house, there is a canal system that runs through the neighborhood. Within this canal community, an independent ecosystem of various wildlife and a family of large, Grey Herring birds live and thrive. Some mornings, you can see the herrings congregating and fishing around the retaining wall on the other side of the iron fence that separate our backyard from the canal. They walk ever so carefully as they stalk their prey of grazing fish who feed on the moss and algae that grows on the canal wall. One herring, we call Simon, was on the hunt that morning. He was perched and watching for his next meal. Suddenly he dove into the water and arose back upon the wall with quite a large fish he had speared with its long, sharp beak. Good Catch, Mr. Herring!

At that same moment, the guardian of the household spotted Simon from the back door. My helpful husband mistook her body language as wanting to go outside to potty, but oh no, that was not the case.

It took no time for that ambitious canine to pass through the slightly opened door to race across the yard to inform Simon that he was not welcome on her side of the iron fence.

The mere sight of the golden border collie sent Simon into enough hysterics that he dropped the fish from his beak and flew off.

It took me a few moments to register the traumatic events as a scene from National Geographic was commencing in my backyard.

In his shock, Simon had abandoned his catch for safety. However, the fish didn't make a lucky return from whence it came, but instead landed on our side of the fence. Instantly. my freshly fluffed, furry friend sought this opportunity to apply the fish's effervescence as her perfume of choice for the day. Her nose found the fish, and she proceeded slowly to roll around on its scaly corpus with each twist and turn of her neck.

A panicked screech of "NOOO!" left my mouth like a racing horse right out of the gate as I try to remove her from the crime scene. Giving this dog a bath to extinguish the fiery aroma that was permanently disintegrating my nose hairs was not on my agenda of today's chore list.

I proceeded to finish my morning cup of coffee and poured another, then warm the shower water to replace her newfound scent with Herbal Essence.

Nevertheless, it doesn't matter how stinky she gets, how much hair is left on my clothes, or even how often she leaves drool in the most high-trafficked areas of the house, she is my treasure. I love her like I stole her, but that is a whole different story.

Do you have any funny pet stories?

#23

Give small gifts of yourself as if to never receive anything in return

Earlier in this book, I state that a single act of kindness can have an 'effect' on those around you. To understand the 'Type of love' that was gifted to you from Above, I advise reading the book "The 5 Love Languages" and examine yourself and your family on how you all 'give' and 'receive' love.

A small summary from this book is that there are 5 Love Languages: Service, Gift Giving, Touch, Affirmation, and Time. I have deducted that my love language it to give and receive love by Acts of Service. My husband and son both give and receive love by Touch. They are both amazing huggers and hand holders. My daughter gives and receives love by the use of her Time. She loves spending time with her friends and family. If any of her friends are in need, she is compelled to go to them and give of her time by listening and comforting them. When she is troubled, she tends to want to be alone with her music or cuddling with me and binge-watching Netflix. Understanding these Love Languages for just my family nourishes and strengthens are love for one another, and that love bleeds out to others that we love and trust outside of our home.

During Christmas (aka the Giving Season), I try to do a standard gift for my special family members and beloved friends. I am a busy mom, and around the holidays, life gets crazier, so standard gifts are a great time saver.

Before the holidays even get started, like right after Halloween, I assess the needs of the family to determine the standard gift. Past gifts have been sweaters, perfume or cologne, Pillow Pets, and a suggested book to read. If the gift is not well received, I encourage the recipient to re-gift because the gift was meant to be either made, bought, and passed on. This year of 2017, the standard gift is a handmade fleece-tie blanket. My sister has stated that you can't have enough of these blankets.

*Did you know that fleece is made from recycled plastic bottles? It's true. You can Google It or try to find the episode from "How It's Made" on the Science Channel about it. I love this show.

Fleece comes in all colors and many patterns and designs for all ages and all genders. The blankets are so easy to make that 'even a caveman can do it'. I like to treat myself to a new pair of scissors because you do a lot of cutting of the strips that will be tied together. Each blanket also gets a standard size: a yard and a half cut from the fabric bolt at the store.

I take a quiet morning and spread the fleece over my bed. The solid color first, then I lay the patterned one on top. I square up the edges, cut off the corners, and start cutting the strips at the far left. After cutting the strips, I light a scented white candle and put on some music. Tying the knots become rhythmic and repetitive. So, when I get into the groove, it takes no time to round all four sides, and I am done. It takes me at most two hours to complete one blanket. I, then fold it, tag it, bag it, and give it! I think of it as time well spent creating something useful and warming with my own hands for someone I love.

How do you show love? How do you receive love? Have you talked to your loved ones about how you want to be loved? John Lennon was right...All you need is love.

...Because, **Love** is the only thing that keeps going from this world into the next.

What is your "Language of Love"?

#24

Good health will be yours for a long time

This subject was bound to come up sooner than later. I received a diagnosis of breast cancer shortly after my own mother passed away in July of 2014. However, I was one of the lucky ones whose cancer was caught early. I had known for at least a year than I had the lump but spending time with my mom was more important. I was also lucky enough to have worked for an amazing oncology clinic for the last five years, so I had connections and a support system already in place. As I lay on my back while the radiologist held pressure on my biopsy site for 45 minutes, we talked about what was coming next.

Apparently, the tumor already had a good blood supply which was not a good sign. I asked his nurse to fax the results of the biopsy to my oncology clinic since I knew the number by heart. After I left the biopsy clinic, I called to make an appointment with Dr. Firstenberg. I would have seen any of the other physicians in the practice because I loved them all and had enjoyed working for them, but BF had a satellite clinic that was closer to my house.

Well, the pathology report said that my tumor was a ductal carcinoma with both estrogen and progesterone receptors. Now, I know the cause. Not my diet…Not my genes…, but stressors in my life had encouraged cancer to grow inside of me.

In my appointment with Dr. Firstenberg, we talked about all my options since I was only a Stage 1, but I already knew what I wanted to do. The lumpectomy was an option along with radiation. Nope, the tumor was ductal which includes the mammary system and nipples, and it all had to go since I was not going to sit across from my beloved physician to talk about these options again later on down the road. Boom, double mastectomy with reconstruction!

We discussed adding Taxotere to my daily routine to block the estrogen and progesterone receptors. Nope, again. It was finally time for that full hysterectomy I had been wanting since having my last child. I have no need for the equipment anymore and was glad to be getting rid of it. Thank you and Drive through! But, the aftermath of that decision would leave me going into early menopause which would consist of hot flashes, weight gain with hair and bone loss. But, I was willing to take those chances over getting cancer again, plus my body would naturally go through this process anyway.

Now that we had a plan, I made an appointment to see my gynecologist to schedule the hysterectomy, and a breast surgeon for an appointment to schedule the mastectomy. Coincidently, my breast surgeon was also making the same choices as me after her own diagnosis of breast cancer. She was at the end of her reconstruction at the time of our consultation. She explained to me her part of the surgery and the plastic surgeon's part of the surgery since I too had elected for reconstruction. However, if I had been older like in my 60s at this time, I would have opted to just be flat chested, but I am not. I was 39, so implants were the way to go. Two surgeries with one hospital visit? Sounds efficient enough for me.

After all that was said and done, the cause and effect of my cancer was gone, but my life was forever changed. I view the disease as being just that…a dis-ease. Plus, I believe it was God's way of slowing me down. During my recoveries from my surgeries, I was able to reconnect with my husband, my kids, my sister, my dad, and My God. When I worked at the oncology clinic, I witnessed that cancer was no longer a death sentence, but a game changer, and now I had experienced it. I no longer live my life in the fast lane. I realized that I was missing too many blessings. I like that I am slower to react to the world because love is patient and love is kind. When I go back for my routine blood work and scans, my sister always asks me if I need her to go with me, so I won't be alone. I tell her that it wouldn't be necessary since I am far from alone when I hit the buildings' front doors.

Now that my mind, body, and spirit have all been realigned, I would like to keep it that way, so I eat more fruit, do more yoga, and write more books. I am not guaranteed to stay cancer-free, but that is up to God, and we will cross the bridge when we come to it.

I would love to thank all my friends and family for their limitless love and support. And of course, my sister, who wore pink every day until I was cancer-free and through the entire month of October because I cannot stand the color pink.

Tell me about your own healthcare hacks.

#25

You will lead a comfortable life

Question: WHO WROTE THIS?

If I had the job to review any and all fortune cookie messages, I would have advised a 'Recalculate' for this one. However, I am sure that the 'creative developer' of this fortune had good intentions, but it seems to me that they might have had too many smoke breaks to 'puff on their magic dragon'. Just to clarify my pessimistic view of this fortune would be that no woman entering, or having been surgically induced into, or aging gracefully with menopause is ever in a state of' 'a comfortable life'. So, let me paint you a picture as I hold in one hand a beloved t-shirt and in the other hand, a recently sharpened pair of scissors to create a more useful tank top for my attire today.

Whether it is hot or cold outside, menopausal women learn to tolerate the unpredictable personal summers that turn their bodies into a hell fire. Night sweats, weight gain, hot flashes, and irritabilities are just some of the symptoms of what is going on inside the body as estrogen is making its dramatic departure. In fact, hot flashes are due to the body not being able to regulate its own temperature in the absence of estrogen. It opens the major arteries, so heat can escape. Those major arteries are located around the heart and lungs, hence all the heat eradiating from the chest and neck.

'Diet', they say to lose the weight, but I wish it were that easy and efficient.

'Take hormone replacement and herbs', they say, but estrogen had caused me to develop breast cancer 4 years ago so that option is out.

'Exercise to stay strong', they say, but when those moments of extreme fatigue set in for a few minutes, you fight for every breathe until it passes.

However, here are some tips and tricks from personal experience that I have found that have eased my suffering.

1. I went to Walmart and purchased a huge box fan and put it by my side of the bed, and I let it run all night. The white noise helps me to sleep, and the air flow is directly on my face and neck just in case my internal heater flairs up while I am blissfully dreaming.
2. I, also, invested in a 'Cool Cloth'. It looks like a Sham-Wow, and you can wet it then apply it around your neck to stay cool after workouts, while you are running, or just being out in the heat of summer. These work very well for hot flashes, too. Just a small tip: Depending on the frequency of use, I would plan to wash it at least once a week.
3. During the summertime, I will take a cold shower. It's quite refreshing.
4. I avoid alcohol at all costs because a simple sip will start a slow and consistent burn for two whole minutes, and ain't nobody got time for that!
5. Like I mentioned in the beginning paragraph, I wear a lot of tank tops. However, I don't like my arms since I have gained a few pounds, so I will cover them up with a jacket, a hoodie, or a cardigan. Something that is easy to take off and put back on.
6. On a more personal note, the 'pause' part of menopause can include the digestive and reproductive systems. I have implemented into my morning coffee a cap full of MiraLAX, so everything comes out A-OK (two thumbs up).

7. Then, I exchanged my water-based personal lubrication gel with the silicone version. Since my body doesn't produce its own lubrication, I needed something a little more substantial (wink, wink).

These little tid-bits have been helpful through this 'season' of womanhood, but the next time I get a fortune similar to this one, I might call the factory and tell them that their guru of messages could be drunk and needs to go home (insert some irritability here).

What sanity hacks have you come across for certain 'seasons' in life?

_____
_____
_____
_____
_____
_____
_____
_____
_____
_____
_____
_____
_____
_____
_____
_____
_____
_____

#26

Follow your heart for success in the coming week

It's January 17th, 2018, and it is 19 degrees outside. I am sitting in front of my fireplace with my faithful canine companion, Maggie. The kids are off to school, and my husband's weekly staff meeting has just wrapped up in the dining room. The house is quiet and clean, but that is only for right now.

Since the beginning of the year, I have been thinking and "feeling" about the goals I would like to achieve in these next 12 months. I use the word "feeling" not in an emotional sense but in a 6th sense. We (as human beings) have a 6th sense built into us to stay in contact with our Creator. He loves us. We all have a purpose, and our purpose is to be the Light that drives away evil from those who have been afflicted with evil. I believe it is that simple, plus I love the anagram K-I-S-S (Keep It Simple Sister).

Nevertheless, I hear in my head things like, "Low and slow. Be patient and wait. But while you are waiting, batch the charcoal soap and make a scrub too. Stockpile the lavender and cinnamon. Save the peppermint and allspice for next Fall. And, keep pace with Nomi to continue working on outcomes of a Fortune Cookie. Yes, you have a cruise in June, but we will cross that bridge of blessings when we come to it." Wow, that was a thought full.

I am a March baby which puts me under the birth sign of Pisces. My intuition is the strongest strength I own. So, naturally, I always follow my heart because that is where my Holy Spirit (aka Jesus's Spirit) lives. The Holy Spirit and I even have a code sign...Its's the number 27.

Case and Point:

1. I was married on the 27th of June, but not on purpose. We wanted to marry on July 4th, but we had a hard time finding anyone to work our wedding on that holiday, so we settled for the Saturday before which fell on the 27th.
2. I got pregnant with my first child at the age of 27 after having a miscarriage at the still young age of 26.
3. My only two children are 27 months apart, and...
4. At my most beloved jobs, my extension at my lab bench was x-2740.

There is no way that coincidence is that specific. However, it did take me 30 years to figure it out and develop a communication with my Creator even though I have always known He was there.

This is not to say that just because I believe my life has been picture perfect. It has not! I have both physical and mental scars from the battles I have fought and the lessons I have learned in just 'being human'. But without these battles and lessons of life, I don't think I would have a book to write. So yeah, I am going to follow my heart because the Holy Spirit that lives there has never let me down, and I encourage you with the small phrase that is printed on the bottom of my journal page, "Trust in the Lord with all your heart and do not rely on your own understanding. In all your ways acknowledge Him, and He shall direct your path." Proverbs 3:5 and 6, Holy Bible.

Find your #27, then follow the Light!

CPSIA information can be obtained
at www.ICGtesting.com
Printed in the USA
FSHW020617151119
64097FS